I0192765

THE
NATURAL
HEALER'S
GUIDE

A UNIVERSAL ENERGY HEALING METHOD

— • —

LLOYD MATTHEW THOMPSON

STARFIELD

THE NATURAL HEALER'S GUIDE
by Lloyd Matthew Thompson
Copyright © 2015 Starfield Press - All Rights Reserved

Paperback ISBN: 978-0692367155

Previously titled THE GALAXY HEALER'S GUIDE
First printing 2013
Second printing 2015
Third printing 2020

Starfield Press
www.StarfieldPress.com
Oklahoma City, OK

Akasha Shore
www.AkashaShore.com

All rights reserved. No part of this publication may be reproduced, distributed, or transmitted in any form or by any means, including photocopying, recording, or other electronic or mechanical methods, without prior written permission of the publisher, except in the case of brief quotations embodied in critical reviews and certain other noncommercial uses permitted by copyright law.

DISCLAIMER: The information in this book does not substitute for medical care. Do not discontinue use of medication, or disregard the advice of your medical professional. This information is a supplement to any current health care treatment, and is not intended to diagnose or cure. Always consult your doctor. The author and publisher of this book are not responsible for the actions of the reader.

Cover design by Lloyd Matthew Thompson

THE
NATURAL
HEALER'S
GUIDE

A UNIVERSAL ENERGY HEALING METHOD

TABLE OF CONTENTS

INTRODUCTION

THIS PLACE IS hurting.

The winds of this planet are shifting and swirling, bringing Change with each passing moment. For so very many, this Change is extremely difficult to handle. Most people have a resistance to change, which causes tension that can easily spiral into energetic and physical dis-ease. From the global level down to the personal level, there is no one and no thing that is not affected by these changes taking place.

But there cannot *not* be these changes.

The changes *must* take place.

Without changing, there would be no... change! Growth and improvement would be eternally at a standstill, forever stagnant, forever wounded.

And what is healing, but changing?

Sometimes a healing is a shifting from a state of dis-ease back to a state of ease. Sometimes it is simply an adjusting to a newness that cannot be reverted back to the way it was before. Sometimes a releasing and purging is needed in order to heal, and sometimes a taking in of energies— whether so-called "positive" or "negative" energies— is needed in order to heal.

In any case, healing is inviting a state of change into our environment. The aim of the healer is to help the client facilitate change within themselves, however needed.

There is nothing magical about being a healer, and healers can be found in every line of work. Even so much as one who offers a smile to someone else could be the exact healer that person needed in that exact moment. Healers are ordinary, every day people.

An *energy* healer is one who is able to access the energy centers of the body directly, assess the need of the situation, and coax the energy into the necessary changes.

Energy healers are also ordinary, every day people. Everyone has the potential to become an energy healer. I believe it is a natural part of the metaphysical aspects each and every one of us carry— aspects more and more people are "awakening" to each day.

This awakening is actually one of the reasons healers are needed in this place. As more and more of our friends and families enter this Change, healers help ease the adjustment as much as possible, and keep the energy flowing. People are aware of the energies in and around their bodies more than ever before, and can quite clearly feel when their energy is unbalanced or unprocessed. It's like an itch they didn't know they had, until they were aware of it, and then they cannot not think about it, feel it, and scratch it.

I believe that those who feel drawn to be healers should be healers, and have access to learn and practice in their own way, at their own pace, in their own time. After so many centuries pinned inside dark boxes, this is now the age of the empowered individual. This is the time we have been waiting for, where the freedom to do things our own way has been claimed, and cannot be denied.

I also believe those "called" to these areas from their deepest Hearts should not have to pay outrageous, unaffordable prices for it. It is the free and unlimited energy of the Universe with which we heal, and it is our free and inherent abilities that make use of this energy to heal ourselves and others. This is the purpose of this healer's guide. The very fact you have opened this book shows that some part of you is drawn to, or curious about energy work as well.

Many healing modalities are quite legitimate and clearly effective, but insist you must be initiated in specific ways in order to use them— yet each one of these make use of the same Universal energy mentioned above, which is the very energy we and all things are made of.

I personally have been "attuned" to the Master level of

the Reiki modality, and used to teach and attune others to this method. Yet the more I grew, and the more I worked with clients and taught classes, the more a restlessness grew within me. I felt this was still far too "boxed in" and regulated— another mirror of the greater institutions around us designed for control and separation. The more I watched the world around me, the more my Heart broke. I sought the root of the pain and unhappiness around me, and found attachment and resistance to change at the core of nearly all healing sessions.

And so I was inspired to convert the energy classes I taught into this healer's guide you now hold.

As we heal ourselves and help others to heal themselves, we are healing the entire Universe. There are layers of meaning to all things, as you will see when you get down to the actual visualizing and interpreting of the energy healing work.

I realize there will be many who will not approve of this book, much less approve of my methods, and that's all right. The method I lay out in these pages is merely *a* method, and by no means meant to be *the* method. It is not even *my* final method, as I myself am constantly learning and growing.

There will also be others who judge this work should be much longer, and much more detailed. Yet I feel that in all things, simplicity remains the most powerful, the most effective. I see absolutely no need to overcomplicate and overanalyze what can only be experienced in the first place. To pin too many labels and rules on anything is to nail it in a coffin. The freedom to learn for yourself and develop your own system is very important in this type of work.

Take what resonates with you, and combine it with what you have already found for yourself. Find your own way. All things begin with self, and can be no other way— what is it that works best for *you?*

My intention is simply to share what I have found in my own journey, as a possible springboard for you to find your own natural way of being a healer. You need no fancy modalities, titles, or certificates to be a healer in this place and time. You need only an open Heart, and an open mind.

See where your own energy wants to go,
not where you think it should go.

Do something because it feels right,
not because it makes sense.

Mary Hayes-Grieco

ENERGY, ENERGY, ENERGY

Energy IS THE STUFF of stuff. All things are made of energy. Hard things, soft things, transparent things, opaque things, wet things, dry things, hot things, cold things— energy. The entire Universe, including your own body and spirit, is nothing but energy.

It is the *vibration* of the energy in a thing that determines its consistency. A lower, slower vibration is more solid, such as a table or door we can knock on. A higher, faster vibration is less solid or even invisible, such as water, the energy that runs through the nerves of your body, or even the energy of those no longer in a physical body. Like the wind, you cannot see some things, but you know they are real and present in ways other than sight. You know electricity and radio airwaves are both quite real, yet you cannot see these with your physical eyes. Your primary physical senses are only capable of registering a certain range of frequencies, though it is energy you are seeing when you look at these objects. Yet there are infinitely more frequencies all around you.

Energy you cannot see, you are able to *feel* through your emotional and physical body. We are all natural energy readers, and we can all read energy. When you walk into a room, you automatically sense the mood of it— if there is tension present, you know it, and if there is an easygoing lightness, you easily feel that as well. You're able to feel your body relax.

In the same way, when you meet another person, you can instantly tell what sort of mood they are in without ever hearing a word from their mouth or observing any of their body language. All this is reading energy.

The invisible energy you feel with your physical body, I call *tangible energy*, though it is not a solid object. This is the type of energy you feel coming through you when giving a healing session, or coming into you as you receive a healing session.

Everyone feels energy differently. Some people feel a cool sensation, while others feel a warm heat spreading. Some people feel tingles, and others report a pressure, as if they were being touched when nothing is physically touching them.

There is no one right way to feel or do anything. You are your own individual, with your own personal symbolism and interpretation system. What you experience will be according to the way you see and understand the world. Never ever let anyone else tell you what should and should not be. There is no way they can speak for anyone but themselves, so why allow *your* self to be based on the opinions and say-so of another?

One way I began learning to sense tangible energy, even before I ever heard of such a thing as energy healing, was by simply holding one hand over the other hand, palms facing. I visualized energy gathering into a ball between my hands, until I could actually feel an energy ball there.

Once I was quite familiar with that sensation and able to create it instantly, I began experimenting with stretching it. How far can I "grow" this between my hands, and still feel it? I discovered I could still feel the energy as far as I could reach, and could even feel it between my hand and the hand of a friend as we separated across the distance of an entire room.

As I continued over time, I found I could also feel energy in and around a variety of physical objects as well, and that there were *variations* in the "signatures" of the energies. Different things felt different ways, though it was clearly all energy I was sensing.

The next natural step to evolve from that point was sensing the distinct energies of my own body, and the bodies of others.

YOUR ENERGY SYSTEM

Y OUR BODY EMITS AN electromagnetic field of energy that extends from your body typically between one to eight feet, depending on your mental, emotional, and physical health. This energy field is referred to as the *Aura*. If you think of the atmosphere around you as an ocean, you could imagine the aura as a protective air bubble surrounding you and allowing you to breathe and survive. When the aura is healthy and vibrant, the flow of energy through the aura field sustains us and keeps us in balance.

Aligned down the center of your physical body and aura are energy centers that regulate your flow of energy, and maintain your balance between the physical and the metaphysical, or spiritual. These energy centers are called *chakras*. "Chakra" is an ancient Sanskrit word meaning "wheel," named for their spinning motion. The chakras are like small galaxies spinning inside the Universe of you, and each galaxy has its own personality.

You have hundreds of chakras throughout your body, but there are seven major, or primary chakras, each with specific properties and colors associated. These energy centers follow your spinal column along an energetic line called the ***Hara Line***. This energetic line is like a rope through your center, continuing down from you deep into Earth, and reaching infinitely up from you to the center of the Universe.

The first chakra is red in color, and known as the ***Root Chakra***, or Base Chakra. It rests at the bottom of your tailbone, and is the center from which your primal survival instincts rise. This is your foundation and connection to the earth. The state of this chakra determines how "grounded" or "floaty" you feel. An out of balance Root Chakra can leave you feeling insecure and disconnected. Your inherited human encoding can also be found in this chakra— the "autopilot" things your body naturally knows how to do.

The second chakra is orange, and called the ***Sacral Chakra***. It is found in the center of your pelvis, and is the center for your desires, creativity, and sexuality. The survival instincts filtering up from your Root Chakra urge you to create and procreate through this chakra, and it is here you determine exactly what your preferences are— what it is you like and don't like. You relate to others through this center, both sexually and platonically. You "brainstorm" in the Sacral Chakra, formulating writing, painting, or any sort of creative problem-solving here. It can be thought of as the imagination center.

Third comes the **Solar Plexus Chakra**. This chakra is yellow, and is slightly above your naval. This is your storehouse of life force energy called **chi**. It is your command center for putting decisions into action, as well as the seat of your ego. When this chakra is out of balance, you may find yourself depressed, unable to make decisions, angry, or selfish. Depending on which way the imbalance has gone, you may find your ego under-inflated (low self-esteem) or over-inflated (egomaniac, full of yourself). In contrast to what we will see in the next chakra, an imbalanced Solar Plexus will quickly divide into "us" and "them." This is one of your most important energy centers to keep an eye on.

Chakra number four is in the center of your chest, and naturally called the **Heart Chakra**. This chakra is green, and quite possibly the most well known chakra, as it is globally accepted the emotions are held in the Heart. A large part of its function is to *process* those emotions, filtering them as needed for your individual requirements and growth, before releasing them back into the ethers. This chakra is where your true compassion and pure Love arises, and where your natural respect for life resides. The Heart knows we are the same life that is all around us, and sees there is no separation.

The fifth chakra is the **Throat Chakra**, which is light blue in color. As the name suggests, this energy center is in the center of your throat. It is your processor for honesty, authenticity, expression, and communication— which includes both listening and speaking up/speaking out. If your Throat Chakra is off balance, you may feel unheard and unseen, powerless, fake, or frustrated.

The *Third Eye Chakra*, or Brow Chakra is the sixth energy center, and is the color of indigo, a deeper purple-blue color. This chakra is in the center of your eyebrows, or a bit above this spot. From this chakra you receive your intuitive insights, knowledge, and visions. When this energy center is "open" and flowing, your clarity and understanding is sharp and true. When your Third Eye is "shut" or "blocked," you may feel confused, disoriented, or foggy.

The seventh and final primary energy center in your body is your *Crown Chakra*. This chakra sits at the top of your head, where your "soft spot" was as an infant. Its color is bright violet or white, and serves as your connection to the Universe, the gateway to All Things. When your Crown Chakra is aligned and connected, you may experience a pure, calm bliss and connectedness to everything around you. You feel your place in Life, and see that all things work together for the best possible outcome. From this center you are able to "download" information from higher vibrations of energy sources, and translate them to this vibrational plane we currently call Home.

These energy centers, and their distinct functions of processing each layer that makes you *you*, are where we begin as energy healers— and healing always begins   with   yourself.

WHY HEALING IS NEEDED

WHEN ANY OF YOUR chakras are not functioning correctly, you become unbalanced. If the energy flow is low or completely blocked, your system cannot operate at maximum capacity. Just as your physical body does not function as intended if you neglect to feed it healthy foods or do not allow it enough sleep and rest, your energy body also begins to exhaust if you do not give it the attention and care it requires.

Some causes of energy blockages and chakra imbalances are negativity, fear, stress, crisis, and fatigue, to name only a few. Holding on to, or "stuffing down," emotions rather than processing and releasing them is another common way the balance can be overthrown, as well as unhealthy attachments to other people, such as ex-lovers or family.

Everyone is empathic to a degree, but some people are even more so than others. If those more empathically sensitive people are not adequately shielded and grounded, they can be easily thrown off balance by absorbing the energies of other people and places, taking the energies on as their own.

If blockages in energy flow continue long enough, they can begin to manifest as illness in your physical body. Emotional bottling-up is one of the leading causes of illness and dis-ease, whether it is anger, sadness, fear, or even happiness, if you are not allowed to express it.

As stated in the introduction, to heal is to assist change. Whether the healing needed is to release pent-up emotions, accept and adjust to a new situation, or relieve a physical pain or injury, it is a change that is being encouraged.

Healing does *not* always mean restoring things to the same state they were before. Healing oftentimes requires accepting that something has changed permanently, such as the loss of a loved one— whether to death, or to an ending of a relationship. Sometimes what is needed for healing is for the client to own their actions, and take responsibility for their part in something that has happened. Each case and reason is different, and there are infinite combinations of events that could occur, creating the need for healing as we go through this ever-changing thing called Life.

BEING AN ENERGY HEALER

AN ENERGY HEALER IS able to access the energy centers of the body, clear them of negative and stagnant energy, refill the chakras with clean energy, realign them, and set them in motion once again at the fullest capacity possible. An energy healer does *not* use his or her own energy to do these things, but instead taps into the Universal energy that All Things are made of. They essentially open themselves up to become a channel or "pipeline" for the pure, primal energy to flow through. They direct this stream toward their client, and toward whatever issue is upsetting their balance.

Some energy healers prefer to do only in-person healings, but others are also able to offer remote healings over distances. Distance energy healings are possible because all things are made of the same energy, and are connected as a whole. Pieces of that whole can be located from any other point. For instance, just as your entire body knows where your pinky toe is, even though your entire body is not *only* the toe, so the Universal energy as a whole can also pinpoint any one specific energy within it, no matter how tiny.

Finding a person remotely and sending healing energy to them works a bit like sending an email. You tell your mail program the email address of the person you want to write, and when you click "Send," it is launched onto the worldwide web and follows the path of the address you entered. Then that person— and **only** that person— now has a message! In a distance healing, you could call up John Doe by essentially saying, "Hello, Universe Operator. Connect me to John, please!" You then use your Third Eye Chakra to "tune in" to the line of energy traced for you, and see what is intuitively revealed to you and what you as a healer can do for John. In reality, this is how energy healing works whether the client is physically in front of you, or three thousand miles away.

Energy healing is much more than simply focusing energy. Although merely opening yourself as a channel for the Universal energy *is* very effective, there is much more responsibility and accountability that comes with working on other people. Keeping yourself clear and impeccable is key to being able to help others, and as an energy healer, you must start right there— with yourself.

All things in your life begin with you. You must put on your own oxygen mask before you will be able to help anyone else put theirs on, just as you must love yourself before you can ever truly love anyone else. If you try to lead others toward healing without "practicing what you preach" yourself, you will simply be the blind leading the blind. A willingness and *readiness* to look at yourself and your own baggage first of all is very necessary.

It is very important to keep yourself as cleared and balanced as possible, so the energy of the Universe can flow through you as unhindered as possible. But all is not lost if you *do* happen to still be processing through something in your own life at the time you are led to hold a healing session for others— the Universe is pure, and as you step aside, the Universe will not only flow where healing is needed in the client, but it will also assist *you* in your own personal situation.

This present moment is where healing begins— right here, right now. All things in your life are taken step by step, breath by breath. Zoom in closer, and you can even see everything is done minute by minute, second by second. If you commit to keeping yourself as clear as possible, moment by moment, day by day, you will find it is very possible to accomplish major changes in yourself, and your life. Commit to be alert for and reject all energies and attitudes that block your flow of energy and send your body toward dis-ease, and commit to embrace and cultivate the energies and attitudes that encourage and enhance your flow of life energy. You are the only one in control of yourself. You choose who and how you want to be.

Anger at others, at the world, or even at your own self is one undesirable energy. To have this energy in your system creates serious blockages in your energy flow and clarity. Even so-called "righteous anger" can muddy your thoughts and actions, even when you have the best of intentions. Letting go of anger brings peace and clarity to the mind, and allows the insights needed to see the best possible action that can be taken in any situation to be revealed.

Worry is another energy that will drag you down very quickly. Worry does no good in helping any situation, and is like drilling small holes in your body and soul. Letting go of worry is a major key in bringing healing to the body. The 8th century Buddhist master Shantideva so beautifully put it, "If it can be changed, then there is no use in worrying. If it cannot be changed, then there is *still* no use in worrying."

Gratefulness and respect are two energies you *do* want to permeate your energy field. Pure thankfulness from your heart, forgiveness, smiling, and offering kind words can both improve the lives of others, and make a difference in your own life. Being thankful brings a natural joy and lightness into your spirit. When you honor the Spirit within all living things, whether humans, plants, or animals, and acknowledge that all things are made of the same energy you yourself are, you open wide the connectivity that is your greatest tool in being an energy healer.

The most important question to ask yourself is **why** you want to be an energy healer. Do you feel "led" to it, as if it is calling to you from your very bones, or is your desire more from a place of ego— the "cool factor" of being an energy worker, and the ability to brag about being so? Is it to accelerate your own healing? Is it to create another avenue for the compassion of your Heart to express itself to others? Complete honesty with yourself, and complete *knowing* of yourself makes a world of difference in this field.

Authenticity is a very important part of being a healer. You must be able to be firmly and strongly secure in yourself and your boundaries. You must be able to tell someone "No" when needed, whether it is to take care of and not overextend yourself, or if it is because you sense they are not truly doing their part of the work in order to heal. If you have difficulty telling anyone no when they are wanting something, you may find yourself backed into a miserable corner, and your own self suffering and in need of healing.

It is not bad to be tired and need a break, but it is bad to know you are worn out and needing to rest, yet continue anyway. You know you would not be giving your best and clearest service, and would be doing neither you nor your client a favor.

If you are approached by someone asking for energy healing, you first "check in" with yourself. Intuitively feel into if this is something you should do or not. If you feel a caution or a "No" for any reason, do not hesitate to say so— and definitely do not feel *guilty* about saying no. The Universe is unlimited in its possibilities, and you are never the one and only last chance for anything anywhere to happen. If not you, then another option will step up to be presented to them. There is *nothing* to feel guilty about.

In the same way, if you *can* do something to help or heal a situation, you do it. But if you *cannot* do anything for the situation, you let it go, and move on. Never *ever* allow guilt to bloom inside you. It is not your job to help everyone, and no one would be able to, even if they tried.

There are also obvious ethics to follow in working with others energetically. There is a deep trust to uphold, so your clients have a pure and safe space that allows them to open to another for assistance in healing. If their vulnerability is taken advantage of for your own ulterior or selfish motives, you will cause them to leave with much more damage than they brought with them to begin with.

There are many different programs of energy healing available, and all methods are merely systems of channeling energy— they are not the energy itself. No one can own the energy of the Universe. Everyone naturally has a connection to the Universal energy, and can be a conduit for healing energy, with or without attunements or initiations into specific healing modalities. If you feel attracted to a specific modality, then by all means pursue that as well. The message here is that you and *only* you have the right to choose the way that is right for you. This applies everywhere, from energy working to selecting which route you take to the grocery store, and all in between.

YOUR PERSONAL GUIDEBOOK

ALL THINGS BEGIN WITH you, and it is no different with energy healing. How will you know what it is you are feeling, unless you know and pay attention to yourself? How will you know what to do if you do not understand what it is you are feeling?

Your first step is to learn how energy feels to you personally, and what it is communicating to you. Everyone has lived their own life and had their own experiences. These experiences color their perceptions; therefore everyone's mind translates everything differently.

Energy is felt in your physical body, as well as in your mind alone.

In the body, many describe the sensations as a tingling or a heat or chill, but you personally could feel *anything*. There is no "right" thing to feel, and even the *same* sensation can mean different things to different people— it all depends on your own personal, built-in guidebook, your navigation system. "Hot" could indicate something is wrong to one person, and that something is right to another person. The only way to discover the translations of your guidebook is to practice and experiment. Begin to pay close attention to your body everywhere you go. How do different places feel to you? Do some places feel heavier, and some lighter? Does anywhere feel creepy or sickening? Where does it feel comfortable and inviting to you?

The difference in places and environments is felt because you and your energy are one vibration frequency, and other places and people are each vibrating at different frequencies. Some of these vibrations are closer to your own frequency, and more compatible, while others are farther from your own.

Pay attention to your body even when you are not thinking about where you are. If a tingle enters your awareness, or a twitch in your muscle, for instance, immediately take a quick stock of where you are and what is going on around you in that very moment. Note it for future reference. Observe as many details as you possibly can. If you later feel the same twitch in the same muscle, then you again observe what is going on around you. Many times, it will be the same or a similar type of situation, and you will then be able to form the translation of, "All right, I see now: when *this* is felt, it often means *that* is happening." With time and observation, you will grow to know yourself and what your personal signals and cues are. Again, no one else can tell you what you should or shouldn't feel.

You are also able to program your own guidebook. If you do not like the signal your body gives you for a certain thing, simply ask your body that it be changed. You can even specify exactly what you'd like to feel for each situation, if you like.

For example, I knew someone who was feeling certain energies as if they were cords pulling at them in various places of their body— pulling so hard it caused them physical pain. It was only this person's indicator that something was going on energetically, yet there was no need for it to hurt them in order to get their attention. They began to talk with their physical body and energy body, communicating that pain was no longer necessary for this sort of alert. The painfulness began to decrease, until the energy pull was still able to be felt, but without the pain.

In addition to being felt in the body, another major way energy is felt is in the mind. I call this "seeing without seeing." This way of sensing energy makes much greater use of your visualization and imagination, and is accomplished using your Third Eye Chakra.

When you use your Third Eye to look at things energetically, it is no different than you see things with your physical eyes. Your eyes register the light bouncing off the "solid" energy of certain frequencies, then feed that information to your brain. Your brain then looks at the information, and compares it to all its previously stored shapes and images. When it finds a match, or near-match, it recalls the label for that match— its "name."

The world of energy works the same way, except you are bypassing the steps of the physical organ sending its sensory perceptions to the nervous system, and then to the brain. Instead, you are using your mind's eye to perceive something directly to the brain. This is much like when you recall a memory of something that happened, or visualize the view from your favorite park bench or meditation space— you can see it clearly in your mind, though it is not physically in front of you in this moment.

Symbolism is the language of energy. Just as your physical sensations are colored by the experiences you've had— and the translations and meanings you've developed from them— your mental visions are also determined by these experiences.

When you set your intention to be shown what is causing your client's dis-ease, and shift your awareness to "see without seeing," you are opening your mind and waiting to receive the image or indication as to where the energy blockage may be. Once you receive the image— the visualization— you may then be able to remove the blocked energy and allow it to flow freely once again, depending on each situation. To move it, you look at the mental image of the block you receive, and visualize it doing whatever the situation requires. Imagine it dissolving, being pulled out, or whatever you think of to change the situation. If you see the block as a cork in their chakra hole, energetically pull the cork out. If you see it as a rope binding the energy center, untie and unwind the rope. Intention and willpower are your greatest tools.

For example, if you receive an image of a snake wrapped around someone, that could mean any number of things. To some, a snake represents harm, yet to others snake represents life, such as on the medical caduceus symbol. But neither of these mean there is a literal snake coiled around your client. The energy will communicate to you in images your mind will translate according to your own personal symbolisms, so you understand what is going on in your own way. You will then be closer to knowing what you may be able to do to help your client.

Some people see no specific images at all, but merely different spots or colors of energy— or even nothing at all. It's all up to you as an individual.

The most important thing is to *trust*. Throw wide your imagination, and do not second-guess what it is you are seeing and doing. Your first thought is your correct thought. Intuition is *not* mental. Your mind is programmed to find the rational and logical, and often cannot easily wrap itself around the concepts of energy and energy work. Trying to operate from the mental level will always trip you up and instill doubts. The only job your mind has in this work is remaining open to the information coming from the emotional and energetic bodies, recognizing the data as the same sort it receives from the physical organs, and translating those signals into images you personally understand. Let yourself experience whatever you experience, and begin to decode your own personal guidebook.

EXPERIENCING ENERGY

As AN ENERGY HEALER, you do *not* use your own energy in healings. It is the energy of the Universe that you draw *through* you to your client. Conducting an energy session should leave you feeling energized as well as the other person. If you use your own personal energy reserve in a healing, you will find yourself exhausted and drained.

To begin practicing feeling energy for yourself, imagine the expanse of the Universe above you. Visualize a shaft of its pure, primal energy coming down and entering your body through your Crown Chakra. You can do or say anything you like to "activate" the flow and communicate with your mind that you are now in a space of working with this greater energy. I have known people who use everything from imagining a faucet handle turning on, to simply saying or thinking, "Energy *on!*"

Gently open yourself to the experience until you feel

the energy at the top of your head. Close your eyes to focus if it helps you. There is no proper thing to do. Once you become aware of it, allow yourself to sit with it fully. How does it feel to you? What sensations can you describe? Do you feel it just in your head, or your entire body? Become familiar with this feeling, so you will always know when your "stream" is activated.

Spend as much time with this— and each of these steps— as you need. Just as there is no right or wrong way to work with energy, there is also no right or wrong pace and progress. You do what you need for you.

When you are comfortable and familiar with the sensation of drawing energy into your Crown Chakra, shift your focus to your shoulders and arms. Feel the energy running into your head, down your arms, and to your hands. Place your hands one over the other, palms facing. Visualize the energy gathering between your hands. Feel the energy beginning to collect and form into a ball. What does it feel like to you? Is it warm? Is it cool? Do you receive a mental image of it? If so, what does it look like?

The more used to physically feeling this energy you get, and are able to start and stop it at will, the more you will be able to experiment with "growing" or "stretching" it. How far can you move your hands apart and still feel the ball of energy?

You are now ready to practice moving the energy.

As with the seeing and receiving of visions with your Third Eye Chakra, the moving of energy is also powered by intention and visualization.

Your thoughts are pure energy, just as everything else, creating waves and vibrations that affect the environment around you, however subtle or obvious their manifested result is. When you imagine something, it is real in one dimension or another. This is why it is extremely important to guard even your private thoughts— for who knows how strongly you may manifest them into *this* reality?

With the energy ball between your hands, open your hands, and hold them palm up, side by side. Focus your attention on the ball, willing it to shift from one palm to the other. Then shift it back. Feel the movement of the energy. How does the flow feel to you? Pay close attention to the sensations you feel, and become familiar with your personal indications of energy movement.

Let loose, have fun, and play around with it. Try anything you think of. Spread your hands farther apart. Juggle the ball higher, behind your back, through a table— anything! To play is to explore and learn.

Try placing your palms together, in "prayer pose," and see what you feel. Can you feel the energy cycling through you with this connection? This is a quick and powerful way to balance your own energy whenever you're in need.

Now, you have the extremely good fortune of having

your own body, which is excellent for providing unlimited energy work experience, so continue on to give— move— energy to yourself. See what you feel as you work with each of your energy centers. Pay close attention to what emotions arise in response at each chakra— but don't just feel them, *look* at them. These feelings and emotions are being brought up in order to be seen, processed, and, if necessary, released. Remember, you are not only doing this to practice feeling and working with energy— you are doing this to heal yourself. You are doing energy healing.

Begin with your Crown Chakra, at the top of your head. Place your hands on or over the energy center, and activate the energy to flow through you. As the energy passes through your hands and into your Crown, how does it feel? How does it feel to your head? How does it feel to your hands? Does the energy feel as if it is coming out of your palm, your fingertips, both, or some other way entirely?

Next, move to your Third Eye Chakra. I have discovered over time that sometimes different people's chakras are slightly higher or lower than the exact traditional textbook position. If you are not sure of your exact energy center, use the sense of feeling energy you've been practicing to pinpoint where it is. Move your hand slowly up and down the general area, feeling for the "ding" of locating it. I feel this as a prick in the back of my head, at my pineal gland, but you will feel your own indication. Once you have found it, and feel it, begin flowing the energy to this chakra as well, paying attention to how it feels, and what emotions arise.

Do the same with each of your energy centers as you move down the line to Throat Chakra, Heart Chakra, Solar Plexus Chakra, Sacral Chakra, and Root Chakra. Spend as much time with each as you feel you need to. Let the energy tell you when it's done and time to move to the next. Experiment with any sort of ideas you get, paying attention to what seems to work best for you, and what does not. Even when you find and settle on an effective method, you can change it later, if you need to. Nothing is set in stone, and, in fact, when working with clients, you will find each situation will call for different measures and methods. A flexibility and openness to "no single set way" is very important in energy work.

Remember to remain open to any visual images you may receive as well— even with yourself. If and when you see something at a certain energy center, take a deep breath, and search within yourself for what this could mean, what it could be showing you. Then feel into whether or not this thing is supposed to be there. If you feel a "no" in response, then you can use your visualization to do anything you imagine to take care of it. Pull out the plug that is blocking the flow, dissolve the stickiness, melt the frozen energy— whatever applies to whatever you see.

When you are done, be very still, and feel how your mind and body now feel as a whole. How does it compare to before you gave yourself an energy session?

You can do this— or any part of this— as often as you like, and whenever you need to. You can never circulate too much energy.

Once you are comfortable with this level of working with energy, and familiar with receiving and interpreting the feedback the energy gives, you are ready for a healing session with another person.

THE ENERGY HEALING SESSION

ENERGY HEALERS DO NOT diagnose or cure others. You are only a channel for life force energy to flow through, a mediator to the healing energies of the Universe, empowering the recipient to heal themselves. As an energy worker, you *never* interfere in the medical treatments of your client, and you absolutely do *not* suggest that anyone discontinue medications or counseling. Energy work is not a substitute for medical care of any kind. It compliments and enhances other forms of treatment and therapy, and can be used while on medication.

Energy healing can help to relieve and heal physical pain, and can also be used to reduce stress, depression, and emotional suffering.

In extreme cases, such as a broken bone, you do not want to run healing energy to the area until after the bones have been set back into place for sure by a doctor. Energy works very quickly, and the tissues may begin to set in the wrong place, causing your client difficulties later on. Always consult a doctor in these cases.

There is no right or wrong way to do a healing session. The important thing is to experiment with what works for you as an individual, and go with that. These directions are only a basic starting point— your purpose is to find *yourself*. You are here to figure out what feels right and works best for *you*. Everyone is different, and you function and do healings in your own unique way. Never get hung up on if you're doing it right or not— that will only block your flow of energy.

Healing energy is holistic in nature, meaning it seeks the root cause of an issue rather than temporarily "slapping a bandage on it." It delves to the deepest corners of the problem, and begins to bring the core issue to the surface for processing.

You cannot heal anyone. Healing is not a simple, passive thing that you can do for anyone, no matter how much you care about them. They must do the work for themselves, and must be ready to heal. If they are not truly ready to release whatever it is causing them dis-ease, the effects will also be temporary. There are many people who are merely after the feel-good high that energy work often induces. If the desire to do the work necessary for themselves is not present, the healing will also not be found. No one else can do their work for them.

Energy work can help shake loose and bring up the

issues that need dealt with most, as well as help instill the courage and empowerment to squarely face these issues.

You can begin a healing energy session on your client the same way you've been practicing on yourself. For ethical reasons, do not actually touch your client during an energy healing session, unless you are a close personal relative or in an intimate relationship with them. The energy can flow through your hands and where it needs to go simply by hovering over the area being healed.

Activate your connection to the Universe, and set the healing energy to flow through you.

Intention is an important driving force in this work. Think about your purpose in doing this session, such as "True healing only for the good of all," or "To purify and clear the energy centers, and remove any blockages revealed." Bring your intentions to mind, and hold your hands over their Crown Chakra, if that is where you wish to— or feel you are to— start.

The Crown Chakra is the direct connection to the Universe. Does this present itself visually to you in some way? Your mind will have its own interpretations, but for me, I see a line I call the *Crown Cord* connecting from the head to the center of the Universe, just like that old tin can telephone line game.

Does the Crown Cord feel tight and strong, or loose and weak? Does it feel jagged or frayed? Be open to any visual that presents itself intuitively to you. Do not limit anything to only a certain set of possibilities—you never know.

Once you get a feel for its state, then follow through with whatever is naturally needed to "repair" it.

Shift your focus to the Crown Chakra itself. What do you find here? Is the energy from the Universe able to flow into their energy center and head freely and strongly? Is it open *too* wide, and need to be toned *down* a bit? Imbalance can go both ways.

The Crown Chakra and the Third Eye Chakra work very closely together. The messages, information, and insights received through the Crown are received and transmitted by the Third Eye. As you move down to inspect their Third Eye, check that the energy coming into their Crown is reaching their Third Eye— their site for Sight.

Next comes their Throat Chakra. If the client has an imbalance or blockage in this energy center, they may be struggling with issues of speaking up for themselves, or speaking the whole truth in certain matters. If their Throat is *over*-inflated, it may be a sign they struggle with keeping their mouth *shut!*

All things must be run through your own intuitive filter— *never* simply assume. Feel into each possibility that intuitively occurs to you, asking yourself simple "yes" or "no" questions, and paying attention to your personal guidebook indicators, until you narrow down what the most likely answer is. For example, you may ask "Is this chakra open too wide?"

and may feel the response for "No." You then ask, "Is this chakra too closed?" and may feel your response for "Yes." You can keep digging and ask, "Is this chakra blocked from another person trying to control them?" You may feel "No," and then ask, "Is this chakra blocked from their own holding themselves back?" and receive a "Yes."

This is what I call the **Pinpoint Method**, and can be used to intuitively find the best way for anything, anywhere.

When you have determined all has been done for their Throat Chakra that is possible, continue to their Heart Chakra.

Many emotions are held in the Heart. This is one of the most important areas of our system. Just as the physical body depends on the physical heart to cycle its blood and remain alive, so does the energetic body depend on the energetic Heart to maintain its cycle of emotions, which is energy.

As this energy center is touched and stirred, these emotions from the past and present may be felt very strongly— by both the client and you. It is very important these feelings be allowed to *be* felt, and to flow their natural course. Emotions are one of the ways our physical and energetic bodies work together to process and filter the energies that collect around us. When they are allowed the space to be experienced and are acknowledged face to face, they are able to perform their job completely, and communicate with our system as a whole. The purging can be gained, and the healing can begin.

When you feel the nudge that work on the Heart is complete for this session, move down to the Solar Plexus Chakra.

Now you have reached the seat of the life force energy. This is the center your client puts everything into action from— their command center. If this center is low on energy, your client may be dealing with issues of low self-esteem and feelings of unworthiness. If you find a rushing surge of energy present in this chakra, your client may have been trying *too* hard to assert their will, which can be expressed as bullying, arrogance, or self-centeredness, to list a few examples. In reality, both cases have to do with low self-esteem. A balanced Solar Plexus is confident and calm in itself, and feels no need to defend, justify, or prove itself to others.

Every intention, habit, and routine is held in this center, so it is important that it be well connected to the other energy centers, and maintain a balance in working with the other chakras. It can easily become a "bully chakra," just as the client can also become a bully to those around them. It's always so amazing to see how everything is a mirror for everything else, from big to small.

Next is the Sacral Chakra. This is the energy center of all creativity, from artwork and writing to sexual activity— all are different forms of creating new life. Your client experiments from this center, and figures out exactly what they do or do not want. If the flow of energy here is clogged in any way, the imaginative ideas that help them creatively find solutions in their lives will also be difficult for them to find.

Again, intuitively follow whatever is needed in order to do what you can for your client, even if it means only pouring the healing energy into the center for a "fill-up."

Finally, continue to the Root Chakra, where your client's grounding and foundation rests. Everything they have accepted and believed in their life compiles this energy center, and is the building block with which they ultimately define themselves. The patterns in this chakra *can* be reprogrammed with determined and self-conscious work. Healing energy sessions are a great help to those actively trying to "re-wire" their conditionings.

The Root also determines your client's balance between this physical world and the world of the higher vibrational energies. If they do not have a secure focus on this physical life as well as the energetic life, they will be "flighty" or absent-minded. Yet if they are *too* grounded in this physical world, they will not be able to connect with their own energy cycles, much less the cycle and flow of the energies around them.

These examples are by no means complete descriptions of everything each chakra does and handles. See the section "YOUR ENERGY SYSTEM" for even more chakra qualities, and by all means do your own research as well— both in person as you work with your own and others' chakras, and by reading books and the internet.

When the session is complete, always remember to release any energetic ties that may have been established between you and your client. Even as you go about your normal daily life, your energy field naturally overlaps with others, affecting and influencing the moods and energy of all involved. When you do energy work on others, cords or attachments to the one you are working on can form, and must be cut and released afterwards, or you may end up "carrying" them around with you, weighing you down with burdens that are not your own.

These attachments can be cut with a simple intention and visualization, such as seeing any ties cut with giant energetic scissors, or even simply saying, "I now cut and release any cords and ties that have established between my client and myself." *Feel* the connection release your energy field. Always remember it is whatever you find that works for you personally.

SOME DEEPER CONCEPTS

THE MORE YOU INTERACT with the healing community, and research thoughts and ideas that come to you, the more you will come across hundreds of different ways of thinking and doing things. Always, *always* remember that, above all, only *you* decide what is or is not for you.

As you continue in your energy healing practice, you will begin to naturally understand things from different levels. The *why* of the methods you develop from following yourself will be revealed over time, which will then lead to further and deeper ideas in a chain reaction of growth.

I want to share a few deeper concepts I've discovered over the years, in hopes they may provide you launching pads to evolve your own practice from— or at the very least provide you with some food for thought.

Energy not only composes all things, each particle of energy is *alive* with its own consciousness at various levels, and this includes so-called "inanimate objects." You are never *making* anything do anything. You are merely working *with* what is already present and alive.

When you honor and respect the life force in all things— from your client to your cat to your coffee pot to your car— you establish a relationship with your environment. You will find things are much more willing to assist you and work with you to meet your needs and desires than you will if you go around trying to bully everything into submission. You are not above anyone or over anything. You are instead an equal with all things, an identical concentration of Universal life force energy. Things work with you, *as* you.

Even the very air around you can become your partner, wrapping around you as you do your healing work, transforming the area into a sacred space both you and your client can sense, and fully open to.

When you are performing an energy healing session, you can visualize your client's system in three different layers, and use the Pinpoint Method to determine the layer in which the dis-ease is located, then trace it deeper from there, if needed.

The first layer of the system is the topmost, most superficial layer, and is the layer I call the ***Bandage Layer***. Merely working on the surface *will* produce results, but they will most likely only be temporary. If the root is not touched at all, the issue will still remain to re-grow over and over. This is the same sort of cure a bandage would have on a blister— it may protect it for a time, but will not have any effect on actually healing it.

Another name for the Bandage Layer could be the Tingle Layer, or the Feel-Good Layer. Many people quickly discover how great energy work can feel on the physical level, and can become almost addicted in a way, seeking the high and buzz of the energy, which can serve as a temporary mask for the real source of the issue, avoiding facing the true cause. This is one form of vampirism.

The purpose of energy healing is to cut through stagnant and built up energy, so the issues that need to be dealt with can be faced head on. I had a client once that requested to stop by for an energy session on their way to a party. I worked on them and sent them on their way, only to hear from them later that evening, very upset because they were having no fun at the party and could only cry and feel sad about a past event in their life. The energy had broken through their emotional walls, and exposed a core issue to be processed and purged. They had been seeking a buzz to take with them to the party, but had instead gotten exactly what energy healing is for. I had had no idea at the time of the session— I had only followed my intuition at each step as usual.

The second layer is the ***Body Layer***. This layer lies deeper than the Bandage Layer, and holds the physical pains of the body. I see this layer as just under the physical skin. Energy work can help relieve the physical pain of the body, but, again, if the deeper root is energetic or emotional in nature, and that root is not touched, the symptom could return again and again.

This layer includes the muscles, organs, bones, and cellular structure. All these can be communicated with energetically and guided with suggestions to begin their shift toward healing— but nothing can ever be *forced* to comply. Everything from the client to the cells themselves must agree to the suggested shifting. The client must be truly ready to do whatever work is necessary to heal.

The **Energy Layer** is the deepest core level. It is here, in the energy body of your client's essence, that the root causes are often found. Emotions, feelings, and energetic encoding that filter up and affect the rest of the system are located here.

The energy body generates and manifests all other aspects of their being. If the flow of energy that sustains the cells of the physical body is blocked or stopped, the physical cells began to crumble, and the body begins to show signs of illness.

This level can only be worked with in the language of feelings and visions. You must sense and feel what is being shown and told, and communicate back to this level in the same language of feeling and vision. I believe this is what the shamans of old were doing when they approached, communicated with, and bargained with the spirits of the land in order to accomplish their goals.

It is important to note here that even though you may

be able to find and see the energy blockages and diseases, you may not always be shown *why* they are there. This may be because it is buried deep and must be peeled back like layers of an onion one by one over time, or it may just simply not be for you to know. Your ego will want to be in control and know all the details, but that is not why you are here. Your place in this work is to act as the channel or mediator for whatever healing energy your client needs in this moment. You will be shown and told only what you need to know— no more, and no less. Your client's healing is ultimately up to them in the first place.

As you work with others in the deeper levels, coaxing their emotional and energetic depths to the surface, you may occasionally have a client that directs the intensity of the emotions they are experiencing at you. It is important to see and realize exactly what is going on, and very important to not take it personally if this does happen. They are simply reacting to and processing their internal struggles, and you happen to be the nearest person to shoot it at. Do not take offense, and definitely do not allow doubt to creep into your own mind from anything they may do or say.

If you feel affected by anything like this happening, simply do some energy work on yourself, ground your Root Chakra, and send the energy that is not yours down into the Earth. This is another reason it is important to know yourself as completely as you can, so any foreign energies may be instantly detected and released.

You may find some blockages you encounter in your

client are not even their own. People more empathically inclined often pick up, absorb, and take on the energy and emotions of others around them. Guiding them to ground and release any energies that do not belong to them, just as you do to release attachments that are not your own, will greatly help clear their energy field.

The chakras of the body are embedded within the Energy Layer, but cross through all layers, cycling and pumping energy to all areas of the being. When healthy and functioning correctly, they spin in a clockwise motion. You may find they are moving very slowly or not moving at all if the energy center is blocked or closed.

I rotate the energy in a *counter*-clockwise motion to "open" each chakra and clear them or refill them, as if I were unscrewing the lid of a jar or opening the shutter of a camera lens. After I receive my indications that the work on the chakra is complete, I rotate the energy back in a clockwise motion to "close," reseal, and set the chakra in full spin once again. Again, you will of course develop whatever visualization is most effective for you personally. Maybe you will simply flip open a lid like a shampoo bottle, or see no lid or covering at all and merely dip your hands into each chakra's energy pool.

If you see colors at each of the chakras— whether the traditional red, orange, yellow, green, blue, indigo, and purple or not— be prepared to expect that they will not always remain these colors the more experienced with energy work you grow. Color is another symbolic way the energy communicates with you, and as different colors are assigned to mean different things in your guidebook, they can shift around to tell you exactly what is going on and what needs to be done.

For example, let's say you see the traditional blue at the Throat Chakra, and the typical green at the Heart Chakra. If you're working at the Throat Chakra, and sense pieces of the green in the Throat, this could be an indication that your client has been working on trying to voice something from their Heart, or that they have *not* been voicing their truth from the Heart.

The energy will give you all manner of clues and insights to detect and decode what is going on. Be open for anything, and do not limit the experience by expecting *anything*.

As you grow more and more familiar with "flowing" and going with whatever the energy naturally leads you to do, you may find your hands automatically moving certain ways. Your fingers may do curious formations, with different fingers pointing or folding in different ways. These hand motions are called **mudras**. They facilitate and enhance the flow of energy leaving the body. Some methods teach specific hand positions, and you can research and try these, if you wish. I have found it is much more effective to follow your own intuition and "listen" to the energy— let it flow *through* you with its own life. If you experience this happening with your hands, simply pay attention to the energy coming through you, and see how it feels stronger or lighter with different mudras.

Quite a few methods of energy healing make use of power symbols as well, drawing them with the finger in the air over the energy centers. These are very effective and useful, but not necessary. It is the intention and the energy with any work that is doing the healing. Symbols and their meanings give your mind a focus point that helps concentrate the energy for an exact intent, and the very fact honor and meaning is energetically poured into a symbol or an icon by millions of people over thousands of years makes it a powerful tool. Rituals are the very same. The action of the ceremony is nothing in itself, but when used as a focal point for intention and energy, it becomes a vehicle for that intention to be manifested.

Anything that receives attention and energy increases in power. This is why traditional folklore warns of acknowledging "demons" or "monsters," because the attention and focus given to them feeds power to that energy. Whether they are "real" or not, your mind can make them real.

Two excellent examples of power fed to symbols over the years are Jesus Christ and the Buddha. Whether these two characters literally existed, were each a single person, or both consist of a conglomerate of characters merged into a single identity, it doesn't matter. The symbol of each and what they represent hold power merely from the millions of people who believe they are what they are. They exist for this reason alone, even if they were never real characters to begin with.

Experiment with and without using power symbols—

both existing ones you come across in research, *or* ones you make up for your own personal use.

Along the same lines as making use of power symbols in energy healing is working with other tools to assist your healing, such as crystals or stones. There are thousands of beautiful and very strong crystals available, from all parts of the world. Each has its own metaphysical and energetic properties, enhancing certain characteristics and healings. Many books are available to research which stones will best compliment the work being done. Some people connect to crystals instantly and feel them strongly, while other do not. I encourage you to play around with different kinds and different sizes, and see what *you* prefer.

Some methods of energy healing also work with "angels" or "spirit guides." This aspect relies completely on you as an individual, and your background foundation. Spirit guides are distinct energies that seem to have "personalities," working with the healer as helpers from a higher vibration. If you read or hear about these things, do not worry or waste time fretting if this does or does not happen with you. Knowing and connecting with your own intuition and guidebook is the most important and most reliable method.

If you *do* become aware of energy guides around you, don't be afraid to invite them to help. Until you are very familiar with the energy signatures of your specific guides, set the intention that only those beings that are present for the highest good of all involved be allowed to assist. Talk to them silently, and listen intuitively for direction or inspiration. Information could be transmitted and instantly just "known," both for what is going on in the client and what can be done to help them.

You will very often feel your healing energy turn itself on as you go about your daily life. It is the pure energy of the Universe, and knows where a concentration of healing is needed most. If you enter a building or environment that needs the lighter vibration of Universal energy, and you are an open channel for that as a healer, the energy can naturally turn on and pour from you as you go about your business.

In fact, you do not even have to do an actual healing session to help others— it can be done silently and privately, wherever you are, and whatever you're doing. One woman I know is a hairdresser, and runs healing energy through her hands as she cuts her customer's hair. Another is a massage therapist, and energy runs from them as they work the physical muscles of their client.

The possibilities are endless, and because everything everywhere is made of the same energy, the opportunities to be a part of changing this hurting planet for the better are countless.

As in all things, there are those who will be more naturally inclined to easily do healing energy work and have stronger intuitive sight than others, in the same way there are people who easily understand advanced mathematics, and those who cannot. Yet those who are not math geniuses are still quite able to understand and calculate basic arithmetic.

Everyone has the ability to heal, and everyone can make a difference in this world as a healer, in whatever form *they* are best.

We are members one of another
so that you cannot injure or help your neighbor
without injuring or helping yourself.

George Bernard Shaw

ABOUT THE AUTHOR

I am Lloyd Matthew Thompson, and I've always been aware of energies my entire life— even while growing up in my strict religious family home of nine children, of which I was the oldest. I've studied energy work in general since 2003, and energy healing specifically since 2007, attaining my Reiki Grand Master level with nationally known energy healer and shaman Phyllis Maxey.

I have been an intuitive reader since 2002, working local metaphysical and spirit fairs, offering energy healing, Tarot card readings, and intuitive artwork readings, which combined my life-long artistic abilities with my intuitive "psychic" abilities.

As meditation and connection with my past lives as monks and medicine men have been unlocked, confirming natural knowledge embedded within my cells and DNA, Shamanic elements have merged and blended with my practice at every step of my journey, creating a well-rounded "First-Aid Kit" for whatever may be presented during an energy work session.

Raised Christian, I have since explored, experienced, and been shaped by many other paths, including Buddhism, Shamanism, Paganism, and New Age. Whether writing, painting, drawing, or teaching, reflections of all these can be found within each body of my work.

I have written for various metaphysical and holistic blogs and magazines, both locally and globally, and have created my own publishing project, *Starfield Press*, (www.StarfieldPress.com).

ALSO BY LLOYD MATTHEW THOMPSON

THE ENERGY OF GOD

WISE ONE: THE SONG OF MANJUSHRI

LIGHTWORKER: A CALL TO AUTHENTICITY

ENERGYWORKER: A CALL TO EMPOWERMENT

THE HEALER: A Novel

ROOT: A Novella

AURA: A Short Story

GOOD NIGHT, NURSE

ENERGY
WORKER

A CALL TO EMPOWERMENT

LLOYD MATTHEW THOMPSON

Look for *Energyworker: A Call to Empowerment*
Only from **Starfield Press**!

www.ingramcontent.com/pod-product-compliance
Lightning Source LLC
Chambersburg PA
CBHW071102040426
42443CB00013B/3378